Kent
TEA ROOM WALKS

Michael Easterbrook

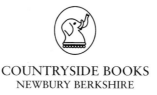

COUNTRYSIDE BOOKS
NEWBURY BERKSHIRE

COUNTRYSIDE BOOKS
3 Catherine Road
Newbury, Berkshire

To view our complete range of books please visit us at
www.countrysidebooks.co.uk

ISBN 978 1 84674 369 6

Dedication
For Florence, Arthur and Alena, our grandchildren

Photographs by Michael Easterbrook

Produced by The Letterworks Ltd., Reading
Designed and Typeset by KT Designs, St Helens
Printed by Holywell Press, Oxford

CONTENTS

Faversham Creek.

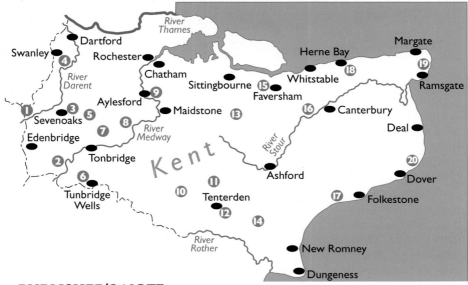

PUBLISHER'S NOTE

We hope that you obtain considerable enjoyment from this book; great care has been taken in its preparation. In order to assist in navigation to the start point of the walk, we have included the nearest postcode, although of course a postcode cannot always deliver you to a precise starting point, especially in rural areas. Although at the time of publication all routes followed public rights of way or permitted paths, diversion orders can be made and permissions withdrawn.

We cannot, of course, be held responsible for such diversion orders or any inaccuracies in the text which result from these or any other changes to the routes, nor any damage which might result from walkers trespassing on private property. We are anxious, though, that all the details covering the walks are kept up to date, and would therefore welcome information from readers which would be relevant to future editions.

The simple sketch maps that accompany the walks in this book are based on notes made by the author whilst surveying the routes on the ground. They are designed to show you how to reach the start and to point out the main features of the overall circuit, and they contain a progression of numbers that relate to the paragraphs of the text.

However, for the benefit of a proper map, we do recommend that you purchase the relevant Ordnance Survey sheet covering your walk. Ordnance Survey maps are widely available, especially through booksellers and local newsagents.

Acknowledgements

I am grateful to David Chambers, Tony Roberts and Val and Craig Easterbrook for their company on some of the walks.

Michael Easterbrook

View to Reculver Towers.

INTRODUCTION

This book enables you to explore the glorious countryside of Kent, while indulging in the traditional pastime of having afternoon tea. You can do a great walk in lovely scenery and feel less guilty as you tuck into a cream tea or a slice of delicious cake, washed down by tea, coffee or a local fruit juice.

The tea rooms featured in this book include one in a lighthouse, one with a famous collection of over 8,000 teapots and several in very old buildings, including stately mansions. Each has its own individual character, some with vintage themes where you are transported to past times and some with very quirky interiors. What they have in common is a fine selection of food, including cream teas, sumptuous cakes and often a range of hot food for colder days. Do check the opening times, as they may be closed on certain days, particularly in winter, and note that some of them only take cash.

The walking routes featured here take you through the variety of scenery that Kent delights in, including bracing walks at the coast, routes alongside rivers and the Royal Military Canal. Others go through medieval country estates with deer parks or explore lovely wooded countryside, with bluebells and other colourful flowers in spring and glorious leaf colours in autumn. Some walks take you past chalk downland, where fragrant thyme, marjoram and other flowers attract butterflies and bees, and where you may spot wild orchids. There is also historical interest in the form of stately homes, ancient churches and bridges, windmills and watermills and medieval timbered houses.

I have suggested places to park but most of the walks are accessible by public transport. A few walks involve fairly steep slopes, so require a higher level of fitness, but you will be rewarded with wonderful views. Some paths can get very muddy, especially after heavy rain, so suitable footwear is needed. There is a sketch map with each walk but it is a good idea to have a copy of the appropriate Ordnance Survey Explorer map with you to provide more detail and to place the walk in context with the surrounding area. I hope you get lots of enjoyment from the walks and the treats awaiting you in the tea rooms.

Michael Easterbrook

The Churchill statue on the village green in Westerham.

1 WESTERHAM

4 miles/6.4km

Terrain There are some gradual inclines, and sections through woodland can be muddy. One stile.

Map OS Explorer 147 Sevenoaks & Tonbridge.

Starting point The Darent car park off the A25 on the eastern edge of Westerham (GR TQ 450542).

How to get there Westerham is on the A25, 4 miles west of Junction 5 of the M25. There are buses from Sevenoaks and Bromley. Sat nav TN16 1TD.

The attractive town of Westerham has historic connections with famous figures such as Winston Churchill and General Wolfe. The walk takes you through heavily-wooded countryside, which is particularly attractive in spring and autumn. You also go along the valley of the infant River Darent and past the site of an Iron Age fort.

The Tea Room

The Tudor Rose tea room is alongside the green and overlooking the statue of Winston Churchill. Breakfasts are served until 11.30am and hot lunches are available from 12noon to 2.30pm. I enjoyed the spiced apple cake. Other delicious choices include lemon cake with lemon curd, Victoria sponge, coffee and walnut and carrot cake, as well as cream teas. Open 9am-4pm Mon-Fri, 8am-5pm Sat, 9am-5pm Sun.
⊕ www.tudor-rosewesterham.co.uk. ☎ 01959 562391.

The Walk

1 From the Darent car park take the path at the far left corner of the car park from the entrance but nearest the main road, signed to the town centre. Go straight across a suburban road to a continuation

of the path then take the path ahead on the left side of the churchyard. Keep just left of the church to reach the main street in Westerham. The **Tudor Rose** tea room is on the right here. From there, cross the green past the statue of Winston Churchill to a bus shelter and cross the main road via the refuge to go up steps opposite and into a passage called **Water Lane**.

2 The path goes between walls and crosses a stream then heads between fences to reach a wooden kissing gate. 10m on from the gate, turn right on a grassy cross-path, with tall trees and gardens on the right. At the end of the field, cross a footbridge over a stream and turn left on a tarmac track, with a large pond on the right. Follow the track past a house on the right and at the corner of its holly hedge take a path off to the right (not the path going straight on past a gate). The path goes gradually uphill between wire fences and, as you ascend, there are lovely views back over Westerham to the North Downs. On the right you may get a glimpse through the trees to the mansion of **Squerryes Court**. Continue past a metal kissing gate with a **Greensand Way** sign, through another gate by a clump of trees then, at a third gate 200m on, go straight over a track and ahead on a path into trees.

3 Keep on this path, which can be muddy, ignoring any side paths. There are occasional marker posts for the **Greensand Way**. After three quarters of a mile you reach a metal kissing gate next to another metal gate. Go straight ahead here on a narrower path to the left of a stone cottage and continue ahead as the track widens and reaches a road. Turn left along the road with care for 200m, then turn left at a **Public Bridleway** sign on a private road to **Hunters Lodge**. Keep on this stony track, straight across a cross-path and, where the track later forks, keep straight ahead on the **Hunters Lodge private road**, going gradually downhill until the track ends by the house. Go straight ahead on a narrower path alongside a wire fence on the left.

4 At the end of the field on the left and just before a wooden fence ahead, turn left through a metal kissing gate. Go slightly diagonally left (11 o'clock) across the grass towards trees then continue ahead alongside the wood. Keep left of a dead tree and ahead with a wire fence and trees on your left. This wooded area on the left includes the ramparts of an **Iron Age fort**, while in the valley on the right runs the **River Darent**, here little more than a stream. Where the trees on the left end, go over a stile to the left of a metal gate and straight ahead on an earth track between wire fences. Ignore a track going off right and keep ahead, walking gradually uphill with trees on the left. At the top of the rise and 100m past a clump of beech trees on the right, turn right through a metal kissing gate in the fence.

5 You are now retracing your steps from the outward journey, soon with a great view ahead to the town as you go downhill. When you reach

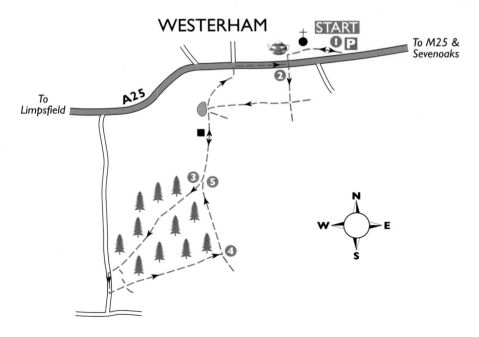

A picturesque pond passed on the walk.

the garden with the holly hedge, turn left past **Park Lodge** and past the large pond on the left. Ignore the footpath on the right that goes over the footbridge used on the outward journey but instead keep ahead for 20m then, just past the entrance to **Redwoods**, go right at a footpath sign. The track goes between hedges, then fences, to reach a narrow road. Turn left between attractive cottages to reach the main street through Westerham then right to reach the tea room and through the churchyard to the car park.

Place of Interest Nearby

Chartwell (National Trust) is the former home of Winston Churchill and has personal mementoes and exhibits of his paintings, plus a large garden. ☎ 01732 868381.

Penshurst Place.

2 PENSHURST
3.25 miles/5.2km

Terrain Some inclines, one slightly steep, no stiles.

Map OS Explorer 147 Sevenoaks & Tonbridge.

Starting point The lay-by near the tea room (GR TQ 526438).

How to get there Penshurst is at the junction of the B2188 and the B2176, 4 miles west of Tonbridge, with the parking lay-by just north of this junction. Sat nav TN11 8DB.

This walk has great views of the large manor house of Penshurst Place, originally built in the 14th century with additions in Tudor times. The route goes through lovely countryside on its estate, passing magnificent oaks and other ancient trees.

The Tea Room

The **Fir Tree House** tea room is in a lovely old Tudor building with a large inglenook fireplace. There is also outdoor seating in the garden. It serves delicious cakes, such as pear and ginger, chocolate and beetroot and spiced honey teabread. Open 2.30pm to 6pm Wed-Sun in the main season, and weekends in March.
☎ 01892 870382.

When this tea room is closed, there is an excellent alternative, passed on the route, the **Porcupine Pantry** at Penshurst Place and you could use the car park there (check opening times).
☎ 01892 870307.

The Walk

❶ With your back to the tea room in the village turn right for 50m to a T-junction by the village hall. Cross the road with care and turn left to go past the **Leicester Arms Hotel** then cross back over the road

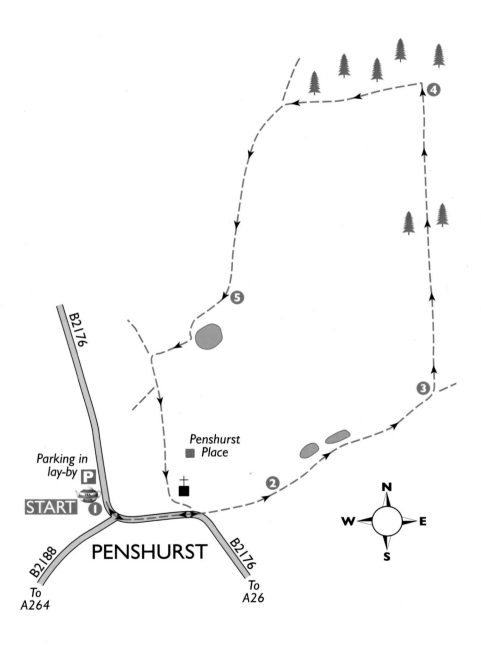

B2176

Parking in
lay-by **P**

START **1**

B2188

PENSHURST

B2176

To
A264

To
A26

Penshurst
Place

5

4

3

2

N
W · E
S

Penshurst Place as seen from the walk.

and keep ahead for 100m (take care, no footway) to go through an archway that forms the entrance to **Penshurst Place and Gardens**. Walk ahead on the private road, with a wall and formal hedge to your left and a glimpse of the lovely gardens through a gate.

2 Where a road goes off to the left keep straight on, unless you wish to visit the house and gardens, gift shop or **Porcupine Pantry** café. You pass two lakes on the left, then 100m past the second leave the road on the left at a fingerpost to go through a gap in a wooden barrier then sharp right on the right side of a field, alongside a hedge. After 70m, go through a gap in a hedge and barrier then go diagonally left (10 o'clock) up a field, passing a large beech tree to your left. As you climb gradually, look back for a great view of the mansion.

3 At the top of the field don't go through the gap stile next to a metal gate but rather turn sharp left to walk between lines of trees, with a hedge on the right. Continue ahead through a gap stile and between more trees. The track goes ahead through a small wood then between wire fences, gradually uphill.

④ Where the field on the left ends, keep ahead for 100m then go left on a broad grassy cross-track to walk along an avenue of plane trees. Stay between the two lines of trees for a quarter of a mile then, where they end, turn left at a marker post to walk downhill on a grassy track between trees, now mainly beech and oak. Go through a pedestrian gate and ahead for 250m between lines of trees to a marker post, then right for 100m to a metal pedestrian gate next to a wider gate. Close to here you can see the remains of the trunk of the historic **Sidney Oak**.

⑤ Keep ahead alongside a wire fence on the left, with a lake beyond. Where the fence curves away left, keep ahead across grass for 150m then go left through a gate in a fence by a sign for the **Penshurst Estate**. Continue on a grassy path past some large old oak trees on the left and with **Penshurst Place** soon visible ahead. When you reach a cricket pitch, keep ahead on a rough track and go straight over a road via pedestrian gates. Go straight ahead across grass, not left on the earth track, with wonderful views of the grand house on the left. At the far left corner of the field, go through a gate and follow a path through the churchyard and between timbered buildings to a road. Turn right, taking care on the road, to return to the tea room and lay-by.

Place of Interest Nearby

Penshurst Place. The huge house has a medieval baron's hall, staterooms, lovely gardens and an adventure playground.
⊕ www.penshurstplace.com. ☎ 01892 870307.

Knole.

3 KNOLE PARK

3.5 miles/5.6km

Terrain This walk is mainly on tarmac, with very gradual slopes and no stiles.

Map OS Explorer 147 Sevenoaks & Tonbridge.

Starting point The car park (charge for non-members) and café at Knole, Sevenoaks (GR TQ 539543).

How to get there Knole is reached by an access road from the A225 in Sevenoaks High Street, ¼ mile south of its junction with the A224. Sevenoaks bus station is ½ mile from the start and the railway station is 1¼ miles away. **Sat nav** TN13 1HU.

Starting at the magnificent Knole, this walk takes you through the lovely deer park that surrounds the mansion. Here you can see herds of fallow and sika deer, plus some impressive old trees. The walk is mainly on tarmac tracks, so can be enjoyed at any time of year. The vast stately home, now under the care of the National Trust, has over 300 rooms.

The Tea Room

The Brewhouse Café at Knole has indoor seating in the beautifully restored old brewhouse and also has outdoor seating, including a roof terrace. There are cream teas, tasty cakes, and hot meals are

The Brewhouse Café at Knole.

available at lunchtime. Open seven days a week, 10am-5pm Feb-Oct, 10am-4pm Nov-Jan. ☎ 01732 462100.

The Walk

1 Facing **Knole** at the gatehouse entrance turn right to walk alongside the front of the house, then the wall of the garden. At the corner of the wall, turn left on a sandy path to walk parallel to the wall but about 40m from it. Where the wall on the left ends, keep ahead and, when you reach a diagonal cross-path and a marker post with red and blue arrows, go straight on for 100m to reach a narrow tarmac road. Turn sharp right on this road, rather than the one that goes straight on, and follow it for half a mile, walking gradually uphill. The road runs between an avenue of old trees, though many of these were felled or damaged by the storm of 1987. The remaining trunks provide homes for woodpeckers, nuthatches and other birds, now including the exotic ring-necked parakeets, whose screeches may be heard as you walk.

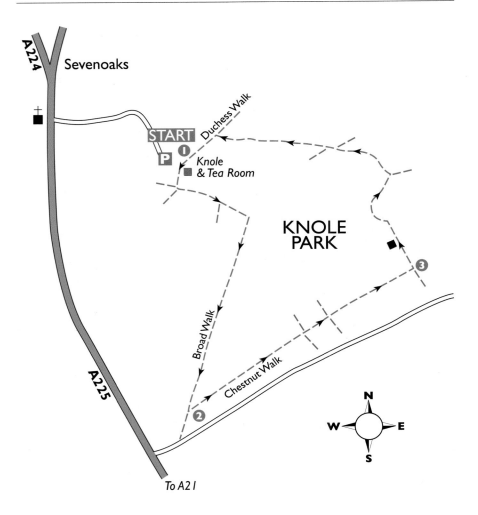

2 Where another tarmac road goes off back to the left, turn left on it. Keep ahead on this road, again with trees alongside, and ignore any paths or narrow roads that go off to the sides. Continue to where the road ends at a T-junction with a narrower tarmac track.

3 Turn left on this track, which soon passes **Keepers Cottage** and a large pond on the left. Follow the road as it bends right then left, keeping aware of golfers on the adjacent course. Stay on the road until

Deer in the park at Knole.

it reaches a crossroads of narrow roads and turn left along an avenue of trees known as the **Duchess Walk** to reach the house, tea room and car park.

Place of Interest Nearby

Knole (National Trust) has historic showrooms, with magnificent furniture and paintings, gatehouse tower and visitor centre.
☎ 01732 462100.

Eynsford Bridge.

4 EYNSFORD

2.75 or 4.5 miles/4.4 or 7.2km

Terrain Some slightly steep slopes, some field paths can be muddy, one stile on longer route.

Map OS Explorers 162 Greenwich & Gravesend and 147 Sevenoaks & Tonbridge.

Starting point The car park in Eynsford High Street (GR TQ 541655). An alternative is to park at Lullingstone Country Park and join the route at Point 5.

How to get there Eynsford is on the A225, 1 mile south of the A20 at Farningham and 2 miles from Junction 3 of the M25. Eynsford station is on the route. Sat nav DA4 0AA.

Starting near the picturesque ford and ancient bridge over the River Darent at Eynsford, this walk goes through lovely countryside in the river valley. This has always been a desirable place to live, as evidenced by the Roman villa that is passed on the route. You will also see the impressive Tudor gatehouse and 15th-century house at Lullingstone Castle. There is also a section alongside the tree-lined river, with the chance of spotting the blue flash of a kingfisher.

The Tea Room

Riverside Tea Room is in a great position alongside the photogenic ford and bridge in Eynsford and the wallpaper with swans reflects this. There is a good choice of afternoon tea menus and some lovely cakes. Earlier in the day a variety of breakfasts are served until 11.30am, while the lunch menu includes soup, salads, quiche, jackets, sandwiches and baguettes. Open 9am-4.30pm Mon-Fri and 9.30am-4pm at weekends.
🌐 www.riverside-tearoom.co.uk
☎ 01322 861551.
There is also a good café at Lullingstone Country Park visitor centre.

The Walk

❶ From the car park, turn right for a few metres then right again to reach the tea room. The walk continues over the bridge next to the ford (take care, no footway), with a white-boarded former mill on the right. Continue alongside the road and **River Darent**, passing **The Plough Inn**, and keep straight on where **Sparepenny Lane** goes off to the right. The road bends left, often with Highland cattle in the field on the left. (If you want to avoid a gradual incline, one stile and a crossing of a railway, the alternative route from here is to continue along the road, taking care as no footway, until you reach the Roman villa then turn left past its car park and follow instructions from Point 5 for a shorter walk.) Otherwise, just past buildings on the right, look for a footpath fingerpost and go up a bank past a bench and diagonally right (2 o'clock) up a field (not the path on the right side of the field). Look back for a good view over **Eynsford**.

❷ Cross a barrier in a hedge then take great care crossing the railway.

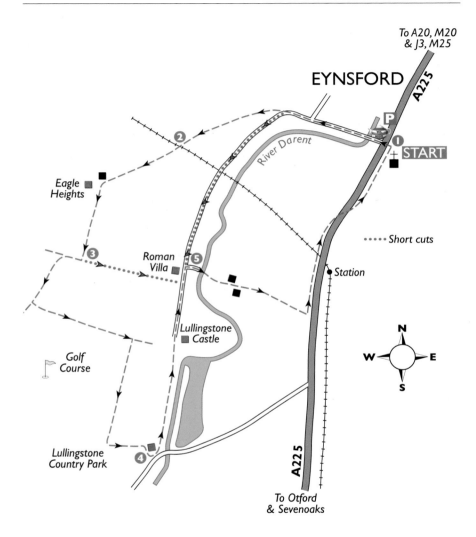

Continue over a stile then ahead up the next field, aiming for the roofs of buildings, with a fine view ahead along the **Darent Valley** and back to the railway viaduct. Go through a gap in a hedge and diagonally left across a small field to a gap in a fence and straight over a narrow concrete road. To the right here is the **Eagle Heights** birds of prey centre. Go ahead across a field, latterly alongside a hedge. At the end of the hedge there are alternative routes.

3 A.) Turn left in front of a line of trees to go downhill and reach a road near the **Roman villa** then turn left and follow instructions from Point 5 *for a shorter walk* or turn right along the road and continue ahead where it ends by **Lullingstone Castle** gatehouse on a riverside path to reach the visitor centre at **Lullingstone Country Park** then retrace your steps to the villa and follow instructions from Point 5.

3 B.) For *the full walk*, turn right in front of the line of trees then, after 100m, turn left through the trees then slightly diagonally right (2 o'clock) on a grassy track that goes to the left of a solitary, skeletal tree and between fields. Some 300m past the tree look for two marker posts on the right of the path and go left here past a broken barrier and on a grassy path with a hedge on the left and a golf course on the right. As you walk downhill, the mansion of **Lullingstone Castle** becomes visible ahead. Near the bottom of the slope the path bends right then, just past where the **Castle gatehouse** can be seen away to the left, go left through a gap next to a metal gate. At the corner of the small wood on the right, turn right alongside the trees (not left towards the gatehouse) on a wide grassy track. Where the trees on your right end, continue ahead for 200m then take the left fork in the track to walk between meadows that are full of wild flowers, including orchids, in summer. The path goes left of a bench and between trees to a fork by

The ford at Eynsford.

a marker post – go right for 30m then left to reach **Lullingstone Park Visitor Centre**.

4 Go past the end of the visitor centre nearest the car park entrance to reach the bank of the **River Darent** and turn left. Follow the tree-lined riverbank, keeping your eyes open for a glimpse of a kingfisher, then through a wooden pedestrian gate and ahead past a green metal barrier. Keep straight ahead on a narrow tarmac road past the impressive crenellated gatehouse at **Lullingstone Castle** and continue along the road until you reach the preserved **Roman villa** on the left.

5 Turn right here on a narrow road past the car park of the villa and cross a bridge over the river. Continue on the rough track past a flint cottage and later past metal gates to reach a main road. Turn left alongside it, soon going under the railway, then keep ahead where the road to **Eynsford Station** goes off on the right. By **Walnut Close** cross to the opposite pavement and continue in your previous direction to pass the old schoolhouse and reach the church, with the tea room and car park on the left.

Places of Interest Nearby

Lullingstone Roman Villa (English Heritage). Discover Roman life within the remains of this affluent Roman home, built from AD 100. ⊕ www.english-heritage.org.uk/lullingstone ☎ 01322 863467.

Lullingstone Castle and World Garden. The house and gatehouse date back to the 15th century and the adjacent World Garden has over 8,000 plants from all over the world. ⊕ www.lullingstonecastle.co.uk ☎ 01322 862114.

Eagle Heights has birds of prey, with regular flying displays, also meerkats and reptiles. ⊕ www.eagleheights.co.uk ☎ 01322 866577.

Ightham Mote.

5 IGHTHAM MOTE

3 miles/4.8km

Terrain This route has some fairly steep inclines, including quite a steep descent, and some paths can be muddy, but there are no stiles.

Map OS Explorer 147 Sevenoaks & Tonbridge

Starting point The car park at the National Trust property of Ightham Mote (charge for non-members) (GR TQ 584535).

How to get there Ightham Mote lies ½ mile south of Ivy Hatch and is reached by minor roads south from the A25 or west from the A227 (follow the brown signs). **Sat nav** TN15 0NT.

Starting at the picturesque moated stone house of Ightham Mote, this route takes you through the lovely wooded countryside on the Greensand Ridge, with wonderful views over the lower ground of the Weald. In spring, the woods are colourful with bluebells, celandines and wood anemones and there are lovely leaf colours in autumn.

The Tea Room _____

The Mote café has the high quality we have come to expect from National Trust restaurants. It is adjacent to the historic house and has indoor and outdoor seating areas. It serves hot lunches in the

middle of the day (12noon-2.30pm) and there is always a fine selection of cakes. Open seven days a week 10am-5pm Feb-Oct, 10am-4pm Nov-Jan. ☎ 01732 810378.

The Walk

1 Go to the end of the car park and walk to the left of the tea room and toilets until you reach a tarmac road. Turn right here to go past the moated house then the road curves left to gates and a road. Go right along the road but, after 40m, turn left on a rough track to pass farm buildings and an oast house on the left. Keep on the track, walking gradually uphill. The bank on the right is colourful with violets, vetches and wild strawberries in spring. At a fork by a marker post, keep right.

2 After another 300m, at a second marker post, turn right up a narrower earth track between hedges to go gradually uphill, later more steeply but with great views looking back to the left. Continue on a path between wire fences, with views on both sides and back as far as the

North Downs in the distance. You pass the huge trunks of venerable oak and ash trees. Continue straight across a cross-track near wooden barriers and up the right side of a grassy field with trees on the right. At the top of the field keep straight ahead on a path through trees for 100m to a cross-path and turn right through trees for 300m to reach a minor road.

❸ Turn left along the road and stay on it, ignoring a bridleway going off right, and later passing houses. Just past the metal gates to **Rooks Hill House**, go left on a bridleway to go steeply downhill under trees on a track that can get very muddy. Keep ahead where the track becomes a road by **Rooks Hill Cottage** then after 150m turn left through a metal kissing gate by a fingerpost. There are more views on the right, then the path goes gradually uphill between fences, with trees on both sides, and through a kissing gate by a National Trust sign. Continue through woodland that has a rather primeval feel and wooded cliffs on the left, taking care as the path has large stones. Later the path opens out, with stunning views on the right.

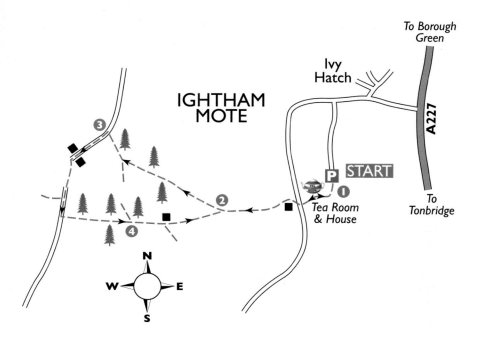

View over the Weald.

4 Keep straight on where a path goes off left by an information board. Later the path bends right and goes down steps, then you turn left to go past the garden of a cottage and continue ahead on the rough track. The track goes gradually downhill then up under trees. In spring, the woods here are carpeted with bluebells, plus white wood anemones and wild garlic and yellow celandines. At the top of the slope, the path used on the outward journey goes off to the left but you keep straight ahead to retrace your steps back to the oast house and road. Turn right for 40m then left through gates to return to the house and car park.

Place of Interest Nearby

Ightham Mote (National Trust). The medieval moated manor house was built from Kentish ragstone almost 700 years ago.
☎ 01732 810378.

Wellington Rocks on Tunbridge Wells Common.

6 TUNBRIDGE WELLS
2 or 3 miles/3.2 or 4.8km

Terrain Much of this walk is on tarmac, with some gradual slopes but no stiles.

Map OS Explorer 147 Sevenoaks & Tonbridge.

Starting point Either Juliets (GR TQ 584389) or the car park in Major Yorks Road (GR TQ 580387) (start walk from Point 6).

How to get there The car park in Major Yorks Road is accessed off the A26, just before its junction with the A267, and this minor road can also be reached from the A264. The tea room is in the High Street, less than ¼ mile from the railway station and buses from surrounding towns stop at the station. Sat nav TN1 1XF (Juliets) or TN2 5TP (Major Yorks Road car park).

Adjacent to the busy town of Tunbridge Wells is the quiet area of The Common, which still has many old trees and is an oasis for wildlife. The route takes you through here and also passes impressive outcrops of sandstone rocks, which are a feature of this area. When you return to the town you walk through The Pantiles, a colonnaded street that has been famous since Regency times, when the chalybeate spring there attracted many visitors to the town for its health-enhancing properties.

The Tea Room

Juliets at 54 High Street serves sumptuous cakes, with speciality teas, coffees and hot chocolates to accompany them. The cakes may include chocolate and raspberry, lemon feather and sensational sunshine cake and, if you can't make a decision, you can get a sharing plate with a tasty selection of six. There are also substantial sandwiches, salads and hot lunches, including fish and vegetarian choices. Open Tues-Sun 8am-5pm.
⊕ www.julietsandmore.com ☎ 01892 522931.

There are also many cafés in The Pantiles, passed on the walk.

The Walk

1 Facing **Juliets** turn left for 50m then right along the cobbled **Castle Street**. Cross a main road with care via a refuge and go up two short sets of steps opposite, straight over a cross-path, and ahead uphill on a tarmac path to the right of a large house. This wooded area includes large oaks and silver birches. Go straight over a cross-path then straight across a narrow road, then immediately take the right fork in the path to go gradually uphill on a wide tarmac path. At the next fork in the path, just past a line of benches at a right angle to the path, take the right fork, soon past a large outcrop of rocks on the right and a cricket pitch on the left. Continue on this path until you reach a main road opposite **Mount Ephraim House**.

2 Cross the road at a zebra crossing then turn left alongside it. Go straight across the end of **Bishops Down Road** and continue alongside the main road, with trees on your right. When you reach where **Major Yorks Road** goes off to the left (signed to the station) you have a choice of routes.

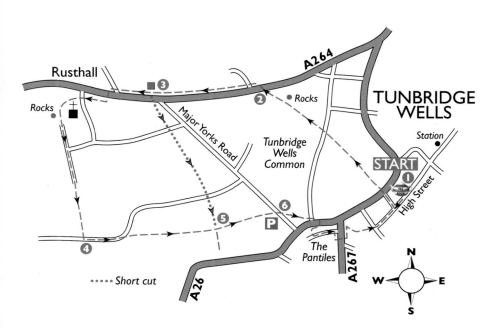

The Pantiles in Tunbridge Wells.

3 *For the shorter walk*, continue for a short distance alongside the main road then 30m before a war memorial in front of the **Spa Hotel** turn left to cross the main road via a refuge. Keep ahead on a tarmac path, with black and white houses to your right. After 200m, go straight across a road that leads into **Nevill Park** then more steeply downhill, soon passing a pond and large white house on the right. Go straight over its drive and continue on a path between trees. After 300m, go straight over **Hungershall Park Road** and keep straight on where the path forks to walk alongside a wooden fence on the right. Later, there is a brick wall on the right – where this ends near a cottage, rejoin the longer walk by turning sharp left on the first of two earth tracks on the left and follow instructions from Point 5.

3 *For the longer walk*, continue alongside the main road past the entrance to the Spa Hotel and later past the entrance to a golf club. Go straight across the end of Rusthall Road but, 30m on, turn left across the main road via a refuge then continue in your previous direction on a path that crosses the drive of **Rusthall Place** and goes into trees. You soon cross a narrow road going into **Nevill Park** then, after 100m, you reach a road leading to **St Paul's Church**. Go left on this road for a short distance then keep right of the church entrance and a former schoolhouse and on a path to the left of an information board for the **Commons**. Keep alongside the churchyard wall as it bends left, then downhill alongside a fence on a path of large blocks of stone that can be slippery when wet. To the right here is an impressive outcrop of rocks and there are good views from the top of them. Continue ahead through a metal barrier then ahead alongside a narrow tree-lined road, with large houses on both sides. Keep ahead where a road goes off left and continue to where the road ends by the last house on the left. Keep straight on here and soon take the right fork in the path to walk alongside a metal fence on the right, with trees on the left.

4 After 300m you reach a road – turn left on it, taking care as there is no footway. Where the road bends left keep straight ahead on the narrow **Cabbage Stalk Lane**, going quite steeply uphill and later passing the large **Coach House** on the left. Later the lane narrows and there is a tall brick wall on the left.

5 At the corner of the wall, go straight ahead (turn left if on the shorter route) on the left of two wide earth tracks. Where the track ends, keep ahead on a narrow tarmac path to pass a car park on the right and past an information board to reach **Major Yorks Road**.

6 Cross with care from near the entrance to the car park then after 10m take the left fork in the tarmac path to go left of a white building, then cross a narrow road and immediately over a main road at a zebra crossing. Turn right for 100m then left down steps into **The Pantiles**. Turn left along the colonnaded street and past the chalybeate spring to a road. Cross via a pedestrian crossing just to the right then go left for 10m and right in front of the **church of King Charles**. After 20m, go left up steps and ahead up a narrow brick road. Go straight across the end of a road by **Pizza Express** and continue ahead uphill for 200m to **Castle Road** and **Juliet's tea room** on the left.

Place of Interest Nearby

Spa Valley Railway operates steam and diesel trains through lovely countryside between Tunbridge Wells West and Eridge.
⊕ www.spavalleyrailway.co.uk ☎ 01892 537715.

Hadlow Tower.

7 HADLOW
3 miles/4.8km

Terrain This walk has only gentle inclines but the paths can be very muddy, particularly after heavy rain in winter, and there are six stiles to negotiate.

Maps OS Explorers 148 Maidstone & the Medway Towns and 136 High Weald.

Starting point The car park at Broadview Garden and garden centre, Hadlow College (GR TQ 628497).

How to get there Hadlow College is just south of Hadlow village and is reached from the A26, 3 miles north-east of Tonbridge. Arriva Bus 7 between Maidstone and Tonbridge/Tunbridge Wells runs along the A26. **Sat nav TN11 0AL.**

The village of Hadlow is set in pleasant countryside and this walk takes you along tracks lined with wild flowers and over streams and infant rivers. There are good views to higher ground and the 170-feet tall Hadlow Tower – a folly built around 1840 – can be seen from miles around.

The Tea Room

Broadview Tea Room at Hadlow College is set on the edge of a lovely garden and in good weather you can sit in an outdoor area surrounded by colourful and fragrant flowers. The interior is light and spacious and serves lovely scones, including a cheese, bacon and chive flavour. There is also a selection of delicious cakes, with breakfasts and lunches available earlier in the day. Open 9am-5pm Mon-Sat, 10am-4pm Sun. ⊕ www.broadviewgardens. co.uk/tea-room ☎ 01732 853286.

The Walk

1 With your back to the entrance to the garden centre and tea room at **Hadlow College**, walk to the entrance of the car park then turn left alongside the road. Keep ahead past the large **Garrad House** on the right, built in 1840, and a school on the left. Continue ahead to pass **Bourne Grange Pavilion** and an equestrian centre on the left then go through a pedestrian gate to the left of a wider wooden gate. Go past stables on the left then, after 100m, go over a stile to the left of a metal gate and walk ahead on a wide track between hedges. After 150m, go over a stile to the right of a metal gate and ahead on a track between fences. To the left is a small wood planted in 1993 to commemorate the 40th year of the reign of Queen Elizabeth II. Keep ahead on the track, ignoring any gates or stiles at the sides, later with fields on the left and views ahead to higher ground. Ignore a kissing gate on the left and continue on the track between hedges, with flowers such as celandines and bluebells alongside in spring. The track crosses two streams and after half a mile reaches a narrow road by houses.

2 Go ahead to the right along the lane and continue on it as it bends right, ignoring footpaths going off on both sides. Pass a bungalow on the left then, 100m on, where the lane bends left, go right over a stile next to wooden gates. Go along the right edge of a field alongside a hedge, with good views on the left to the **Greensand Ridge** and a large white house called **Oxenhoath**. Cross a footbridge over the narrow **River Bourne**, over a stile and straight across a smaller field. Go over

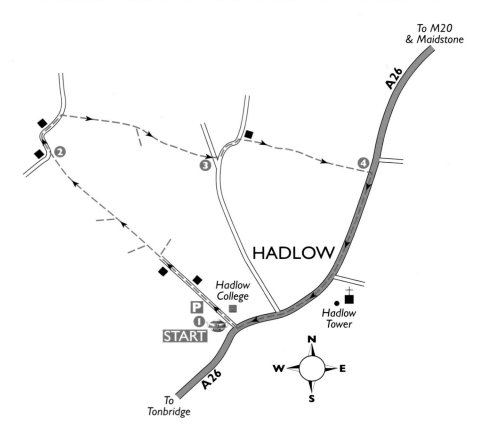

a stile to the right of metal gates then go straight ahead across a field (don't take the right fork in the path that skirts trees and leads to a footbridge). Cross a ditch via a grassy track, 40m to the left of the footbridge, then go slightly diagonally left (11 o'clock) ahead up a large field. **Hadlow Tower** becomes visible ahead in the distance as you go straight across a stony track and continue towards houses. At the end of the field go through a kissing gate in a hedge, 20m right of wooden gates, taking care as you emerge onto a road.

❸ Go straight over this road then, 10m on, turn left along a narrow lane, signed to **The Common**. The lane bends right by **Broom House** then, after 100m where it bends left, take a path on the right, just before a terrace of white-painted houses. After 30m, go through a metal gate

View to higher ground and Oxenhoath House.

and ahead on the left side of a field. At the end of the field the path goes through scrub to cross a stile at the left end of a tall green metal fence then, 20m on, go left through a metal kissing gate and, after another 20m, turn right on a path alongside a wire fence and hedge on the left. Keep on this path for a quarter of a mile, later with houses on the right, to reach a main road.

4 Turn right alongside the road and follow it for three quarters of a mile, ignoring any side roads. You go through **Hadlow** village, passing a road leading to the ancient church and later the entrance to **Hadlow Tower** (private). Finally, the path alongside the main road crosses the **River Bourne** and you turn right into the entrance to **Hadlow College**, soon with the tea room and car park on the left.

Place of Interest Nearby

Hop Farm Family Park has an animal farm, children's play areas and museums, all set in a large array of Victorian oast houses.
⊕ www.hopfarm.co.uk ☎ 01622 872068.

Boats moored on the river at Yalding.

8 YALDING

5.5 miles/8.8km

Terrain This route is mainly flat, with one gradual slope and two stiles. The riverside path can be muddy after rain.

Map OS Explorers 148 Maidstone & the Medway Towns and 136 High Weald.

Starting point The Lees car park in Hampstead Lane, Yalding (GR TQ 691497).

How to get there The car park and adjacent café are reached off the B2162, ½ mile from the junction of the B2015 with the A228 and ½ mile south-west of Yalding village. Yalding and Wateringbury stations are very close to the route and Arriva Bus 6 between Maidstone and Tunbridge Wells runs through Wateringbury and Nettlestead. **Sat nav** ME18 6HG.

Riverside views form a large part of this walk, with the associated birds and flowers and lots of boats to be admired, either moored or moving serenely along the river. You will also see ancient bridges, houses and church, plus a lovely millpond.

The Tea Room

Amazingly, **Teapot Island tea room** has a collection of over 8,250 teapots, making it a Guinness World Record holder. You can gaze at some of these as you eat, while most are in a special exhibition room (small charge). There is also an outdoor eating area overlooking the river. As well as cream teas and tempting cakes there is a range of breakfasts, main courses and desserts to choose from. Open mid-Jan to mid-Dec, 10am-4pm Mon-Fri, 9am-5pm Sat-Sun. ⊕ www.teapotisland.co.uk ☎ 01622 814541.

Teapot Island.

The Walk

1 If parked in the car park, on the right side from the entrance a path leads over a footbridge to **Teapot Island**. From the front of the café go ahead to the right of the outdoor seating area on a tarmac road that crosses the river and weir, with a fine view of the ancient bridge. On reaching a road turn left alongside it, soon with the river on the left. After half a mile you cross another bridge over the river then, 80m on, cross the road with care and, just before a new housing development, pass a metal gate at a footpath fingerpost.

2 The path initially runs between a wall and the river, which has boats moored on it. Keep right where the path forks to stay alongside the river, which soon branches and has more boat moorings. As you continue on the riverside path there are flowers such as purple loosestrife to be seen in summer and the large white **Kenward House** is visible in the distance across the river. You pass fields on the left and there are tall trees with large bunches of mistletoe. Continue through a belt of trees, still alongside the river, and when you emerge from them there is a fine view ahead to **Nettlestead Place**, a medieval house. Keep ahead, soon between a railway line and the river, and stay on this path until you reach another marina of moored boats. Walk past them on a track, past a gate, then up to a road on the left side of a bridge. (If you wish to avoid a gradual incline and two stiles retrace your steps back to the start from here.)

3 Turn left across the railway crossing, noticing the old signal box, to reach a main road on a bend. Go ahead past the entrance road to **Wateringbury station**, then use a pedestrian crossing to cross the road and continue uphill alongside the road. About 30m before **Warden Mill Close**, go left at a **Restricted Byway fingerpost** on a rough track that soon bends right, with an orchard behind the hedge on the right. On reaching a narrow road opposite an oast house turn left, then where the road bends right by a former millhouse keep ahead to the left of a large millpond. Follow this narrow road as it bends left, ignoring a path going ahead. You pass a large house with a walled garden, then the road ends at another house on the right. Go ahead through a wooden gate and shortly a pedestrian gate, then ahead on the left side of a field, with a wire fence on the left and views along the valley. Ignore a footpath going off left and continue ahead, then

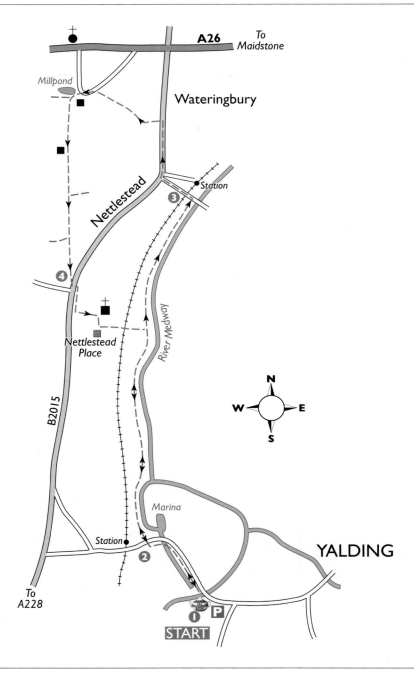

through a gap at the end of a hedge and ahead on the left edge of a smaller field. At the far left corner of the field, go ahead past two metal barriers and on a tarmac path between a fence and houses on the left and a hedge on the right. Keep on this path, later between hedges and with a recreation ground on the left, then keep ahead on the right side of a wooden fence on a path between the fence and a hedge.

4 On reaching a main road, cross with care and turn right on the opposite pavement. After 250m, turn left through the lychgate of **St Mary's Church** to follow a path to the church, which has some fine old memorials and stained glass. Turn right at the church porch then left alongside a wall, through a stone arch and down the right side of a field. To the right are the gardens of **Nettlestead Place**. Cross the railway with care via two stiles and turn right on the riverside path. Retrace your steps back to the marina at Yalding then left at the road to return to the café and car park.

Place of Interest Nearby

Hop Farm Family Park has an animal farm, children's play areas and museums, all set in a large array of Victorian oast houses.
⊕ www.hopfarm.co.uk ☎ 01622 872068.

View to the medieval Nettlestead Place.

The ancient bridge at Aylesford.

9 AYLESFORD
3.5 miles/5.6km

Terrain Mainly flat with no stiles on main route (2 on short cut).

Map OS Explorer 148 Maidstone & the Medway Towns.

Starting point The car parks on the edge of the village just north of the bridge (GR TQ 732588).

How to get there Aylesford can be reached from the A20 near Junction 5 of the M20 or via a B road from Junction 6 of the M20. Arriva bus 155 between Maidstone and Rochester runs through the village and Aylesford railway station is ¾ mile from the start. **Sat nav ME20 7AU.**

This walk starts in the historic village of Aylesford, with its medieval ragstone bridge and ancient church, and takes you along the valley of the River Medway to the lock at Allington. Here you can see some interesting barges and boats moored on the river before returning alongside the river, with swans, ducks and geese to see.

The Tea Room

The Village Pantry is close to the junction of Forstal Road with Rochester Road and the High Street, where there are many old buildings. The interior has some vintage touches and there is

also a courtyard garden. At lunchtime you can get an Aylesford rarebit and other selections such as smashed avocado with free range eggs, while breakfasts are served all day. You can enjoy pancakes or a slice of cake, including Kentish apple. Open 8.30am-4pm Mon-Sat, closed Sunday. ☎ 01622 792673.

The Walk

1 From the car park walk back to the road and across the bridge over the **River Medway**. To the right here is the iconic view of the ancient ragstone bridge, with the church and village behind, that has featured on many calendars. Over the bridge turn left at the end of the wall on the left at a fingerpost for the **Medway Valley Walk**. After 30m on a tarmac track, turn right on a narrow path between the river on the left and houses on the right. After 400m, turn right to cross a railway with care at a pedestrian crossing then go immediately left on a footpath running parallel to the railway. After 300m, the path turns sharp right, still with a wooden fence on the right, then where the fence ends turn left as the path runs through the edge of a small wood.

2 Where the trees end keep ahead between fields, with the M20 motorway visible to the right. Soon the path runs alongside trees on the left. About 100m before the motorway, go left into the wood at a marker post then, after 150m, turn left on a cross-track for 50m and right on a tarmac track that crosses over the motorway. Keep on this track as it bends left then becomes a narrow path alongside the motorway, with trees on the right. Pass a **World War II pillbox** and continue downhill under trees, now with a railway on the left.

3 (Look on the left for a crossing over the railway via stiles – use this if you want to *shorten the walk* by half a mile. Once across the railway turn right on a path for 100m to reach a track and go straight ahead before bending right past a boatyard on the left. Turn left at a red footpath sign to go down steps to the riverbank then ahead through trees to reach **Allington Lock**.)

Alternatively, *for the full walk*, keep ahead on the path between fences, later crossing two footbridges, with a quarry on the right. When you reach a road turn left on a bridge over the railway and continue with care, as no footway, to a T-junction by a gatehouse for **Allington Castle**. Turn left past the ancient **Allington Church**, now a dwelling, and downhill to reach **Allington Lock**.

4 Go ahead over the lock using the footbridge then turn right and cross the river via an elevated footbridge, from which there are great views of the boats, including old sailing barges, which are moored on the river. Once over the river the walk turns back to the left, though you may want to go right for a close view of the boats or to visit the **Malta Inn** or **Kent Life**. After 200m, there are two parallel paths, one alongside the river and the other, better-surfaced, path a short distance away. The paths soon converge and you stay alongside the river to

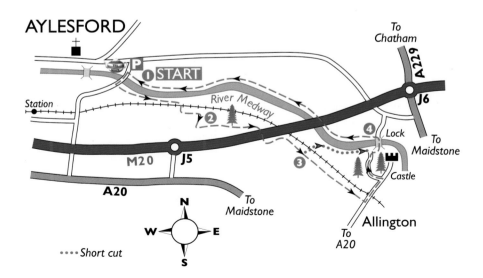

Boats moored at Allington Lock.

pass under the motorway. Later the path has a wood-boarded section – soon after this, take care if you have children or dogs with you as there is an unfenced section of riverbank. The path passes industrial units then finally meadows with marshy areas and over a footbridge before reaching the car parks at **Aylesford**.

Place of Interest Nearby

Kent Life has a vintage village, indoor and outdoor play areas, farmyard animals, meerkats and owls.
⊕ www.kentlife.org.uk ☎ 01622 763936.

The smock mill towers over the town of Cranbrook.

10 CRANBROOK

3.75 miles/6km

Terrain The slopes on this walk are gentle but the field paths can be muddy and there is one stile.

Map OS Explorer 136 High Weald.

Starting point The car park off the High Street (GR TQ 775360).

How to get there Cranbrook is just off the A229, between Staplehurst and Hawkhurst. There are buses from Maidstone, Hawkhurst and Tunbridge Wells. Sat nav TN17 3DQ.

The attractive market town of Cranbrook has a well-preserved windmill, visible at several points on the walk, and the fine church is also passed on the route. The route takes you through the lovely wooded countryside that surrounds the town, before returning past Cranbrook School, which was established in the 16th century.

The Tea Room _____

Waterloo House Tearooms & Antiques in Waterloo Road has a good selection of food and drink in pleasant surroundings. There is a varied menu for breakfast, brunch and lunch along with a selection of delicious cakes, teas and coffees. Open 9am-5pm Mon-Sat, 10am-4pm Sun.

⊕ www.waterloohouseantiquitea.com ☎ 01580 713802

The Walk

1 From the car park, walk back to the main street and turn right. Where the road turns sharp right, turn left in front of the **Weald Information Centre** in **Vestry Hall** to enter the churchyard. Take the paved path that goes to the left of the church and, at the end of the churchyard, keep ahead on a rough path alongside the churchyard wall. Keep alongside a wall and hedge on the right, with a playing field on your left, as the path bends right, then finally down steps to a main road.

2 Go straight across with care and up a couple of steps then ahead on a path between hedges. Behind the tall wire fence on the left is parkland with some magnificent trees. Keep ahead through a gate and continue alongside the wire fence, with fields on the right and fine views over the heavily wooded countryside. Keep straight on where a path goes off left through a gate in the fence and, 50m on, keep straight ahead, now on a tarmac path, where a path goes off to the right by an oak tree. After half a mile, the track bends right to enter a wood by wooden gates but you leave it here on the left through a wooden pedestrian gate at a low concrete footpath sign. Go ahead on a path between fences through a wood. Leave the wood via a metal kissing gate and take the right fork in the path to go slightly diagonally right (2 o'clock) up the field to another kissing gate and down steps to a narrow tarmac road.

3 Turn right along the road, soon past houses and through a metal gate or over the stile next to it. Continue for 50m then, just before a brick building on the left and opposite stables, go left past a metal barrier on a path that winds through trees. Go through two gates in quick succession, then ahead for 30m to the corner of a wire fence and ahead across a field to another kissing gate. Continue to the right on a rough track, with a hedge and later a wood on the right. The track continues ahead between fields, past corrugated metal barns on the left, then bends left to go to the right of a house and goes through a wood and over a stream. Follow the track, which is now concrete, as it bends sharp right, soon with a line of oak trees on the left, until it reaches a road.

4 Turn right along the roadside verge for 100m then go right at a footpath fingerpost, through a kissing gate and ahead across a field

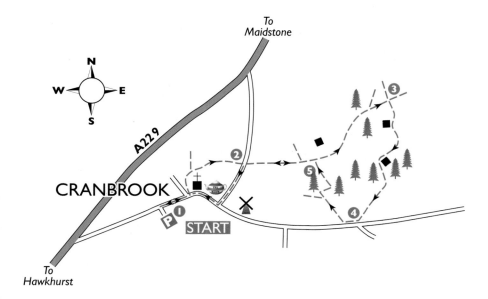

(11 o'clock) to a clump of trees projecting out into the field. Keep left of these trees then through a gap in a line of trees and ahead on the right edge of a field, with trees on your right. At the end of the field keep ahead on a path into trees and over a footbridge across a stream, then up a slope through trees and scrub to a field. Go right

St Dunstan's Church in Cranbrook.

here alongside trees on your right but, after 100m, turn sharp left (no path marker) to go gradually uphill on the right side of a field, with a broken hedge line on the right. After 300m, you reach the wire fence and path from the outward journey.

5 Turn left along the path alongside the fence until you reach the main road. Cross with care then turn left on the pavement alongside the road. You pass some attractive houses and the interesting buildings of **Cranbrook School**, and there is a view of **Cranbrook Windmill** through a gap on the left. When you reach a road junction keep right to the teashop and other cafés (or to the left for a better view of the windmill). Turn left near the information centre to return to the car park.

Place of Interest Nearby

Sissinghurst Castle Garden (National Trust) is one of the most famous gardens in England, set around an ancient tower.
☎ 01580 710700.

Cranbrook Windmill, the tallest surviving smock mill in the British Isles, is open on Saturdays and some Sundays during the summer.
⊕ www.unionmill.org.uk ☎ 01580 714557.

Biddenden village.

11 BIDDENDEN
3.5 miles/5.6km

Terrain This route is mainly flat and partly on lanes. There are four stiles.

Map OS Explorer 137 Ashford.

Starting point The car park behind the post office, near the junction of the A274 and A262. If this car park is full there is a larger one 300m south off the A262, at the Recreation Ground, reached by a drive off Old Mill Court (GR TQ 852384).

How to get there Biddenden lies at the junction of the A262 and A274 between Headcorn and Tenterden. Arriva Bus 12 between Maidstone and Tenterden runs through the village. Sat nav TN27 8AL (post office) or TN27 8BB (Recreation Ground).

Biddenden is a lovely village where the main street is lined with medieval houses and has pavements of Bethersden marble. The wealth of the village at that time came from the cloth-making industry and this is also reflected in the magnificent church. From here the route takes you through pleasant countryside, dotted with many ponds, and along lanes lined with wild flowers. You also go past other old houses and the church.

The Tea Room

Amazingly for a village of its size, Biddenden has two excellent tea rooms. The Bakehouse is opposite the post office in an old building that has dried hops draped over the beams, and rustic tables. There are cream teas, delicious cakes such as lemon or Victoria sponge and all day breakfasts. You can also get hot lunches. Open 9am-4pm Tues to Sat. ☎ 01580 292270.

The Bakehouse.

The Tiny Teapot is along the same street towards the church. It is also in a very old building and serves cakes, scones and light lunches. Conveniently it is open on days when The Bakehouse is closed, open Thurs-Mon 9am-4pm. ☎ 01580 291879.

The Walk

1 From the car park behind the post office, go out of its entrance and turn right for 20m to cross the main road via a refuge (if coming from the car park at the **Recreation Ground** walk back to the main road and turn left for 200m to this refuge). Turn left for 100m then, just past **Avery Cottage**, turn right at a footpath sign on a stone path between houses. Keep ahead as the path becomes earth to go to the right of a fence behind gardens and, where the fence ends, go through a metal pedestrian gate on the left, not on the path straight ahead. Go slightly diagonally right (2 o'clock) across a field to a metal gate near the far right corner then ahead alongside a hedge that skirts a pond, bending right then left. After 150m, go right through a metal kissing gate in the hedge then keep alongside the hedge on the left for 40m and over a stile on the left. The path forks here – keep straight ahead alongside the hedge on the left then between two large ponds via a stile and ahead alongside a fence and hedge on the left to a kissing gate. Continue ahead across a field to a kissing gate and ahead across the next field to another. Keep ahead, aiming just right of a large house, to reach a pedestrian gate to the right of a wider gate and onto a lane.

2 Turn left on the lane, passing **River Hall** with its bell turret, then, after 500m, turn left on another lane at a junction. Keep on this lane, with primroses and celandines on the verges in spring, for half a mile, finally passing a lovely timbered house to reach a main road. Cross with care and turn left on the pavement past houses. Just past an **Indian restaurant** go right at a fingerpost on a path between a garden and a fence to reach a pedestrian gate and across a small field to another. Continue ahead past another pond on the left and through a

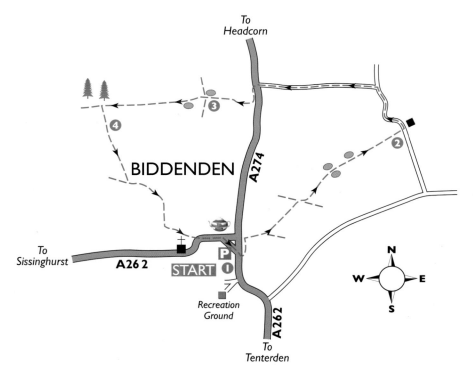

line of trees near the left edge then, 30m on, turn left over a footbridge and stile. Cross the former trackbed of a railway to another stile then go sharp right for 50m to a metal pedestrian gate and ahead for 80m to another gate by a footbridge.

A timbered house passed on the walk.

❸ Don't go through this gate but instead turn left alongside a wire fence and hedge on the right side of a field. At a marker post on the right, keep straight on to go to the right of a pond then through a wooden pedestrian gate and ahead near the right side of a field. Continue through a gap in a hedge and ahead across the next field, with a vineyard behind the hedge on the right. Go through a metal kissing gate and ahead on the right edge of the next field to a footbridge and kissing gate. Keep to the right edge of the next field but, after 150m, look for a marker post behind the fence on the right and go sharp left across the field for 100m to a pedestrian gate and footbridge over a stream.

❹ Go slightly diagonally left (11 o'clock) across a long field towards houses, keeping just left of trees around a pond in the middle of the field. At the far left corner, go over a footbridge, through a pedestrian gate, and ahead on a path between wire fences to a kissing gate by a pond. Continue ahead between garden fences, with **Biddenden Church** now visible ahead, then alongside a road between houses. Just past a children's playground on the left, go left across grass for 100m to a marker post near a large oak, then turn right on a path, soon alongside a wooden fence. At a junction with a tarmac path turn left over a stream towards the church. Cross a road then walk ahead on a path through the churchyard, keeping ahead past the church and through the lychgate. Continue ahead alongside a road to reach the tea rooms and car park.

Places of Interest Nearby

Biddenden Vineyards produce wine, cider and apple juice.
⊕ www.biddendenvineyards.com ☎ 01580 291726.

Sissinghurst Castle Garden (National Trust) is one of the most famous gardens in England, set around an ancient tower.
☎ 01580 710700.

Apple orchard passed on the walk.

12 TENTERDEN

2.5 miles/4km

Terrain This route is fairly flat and mostly on good surfaces. There are no stiles.

Map OS Explorer 125 Romney Marsh.

Starting point The tea room at 29 High Street (GR TQ 885334); the nearest car park is in Recreation Ground Road (GR TQ 886334).

How to get there Tenterden is on the A28, 11 miles south-west of Ashford. There are buses to the town from Ashford, Maidstone and Tunbridge Wells. Sat nav TN30 6BN (car park).

The lovely market town of Tenterden has a wide, tree-lined street, historic buildings, including a fine church, and a steam railway. This walk takes you through pleasant countryside south of the town, with distant views of the tall church tower. You will also see the large trees of traditional apple orchards.

The Tea Room

The **Lemon Tree** occupies a lovely timbered building, dating back to the 14th century. Here, surrounded by beams, you can get some great food. As well as cream teas you can have a high tea with Welsh rarebit muffin and there are sumptuous cakes, such as lemon cream pie with raspberry coulis and berries. Hot lunches, including roasts, and breakfasts are also available. Open 9am-5pm every day. ⊕ www.lemontreetenterden.co.uk ☎ 01580 763381.

The Walk

❶ With your back to **The Lemon Tree** go left for 30m, then turn left between **Nationwide** and **Café Rouge** into a passageway called **Bells Lane**. Continue between pretty cottages and look back for a good view to the church. Go straight ahead, with allotments on the left, and keep straight on where a footpath goes off to the right. Continue past houses on the left and where they end keep ahead on a tarmac path with a tall hedge on your right. Keep ahead on this tarmac path (when

I did the walk it passed through a site where new houses were being built), later with a hedge on the left and a field on the right. After a quarter of a mile you reach a road opposite **Tenterden Cricket Club**.

2 Go sharp left here along a rough road, passing **Hopes Grove Nurseries**. Continue ahead on the road which, after the large **Hopes Grove house**, becomes a rough track. Immediately before a sign for **Belcot Manor Farm** go left past a metal gate on a narrow path between a low fence on the right and hedge on the left. You pass a large farm pond, patrolled by dragonflies in summer, behind the fence, then the path continues between a wire fence on the left and hedge on the right. In high summer you can see colourful wild flowers here, such as purple knapweed and tufted vetch and yellow fleabane and meadow vetchling. After a quarter of a mile the track goes through a belt of trees with a stream in a deep gorge, then gradually uphill, with a hedge on the left.

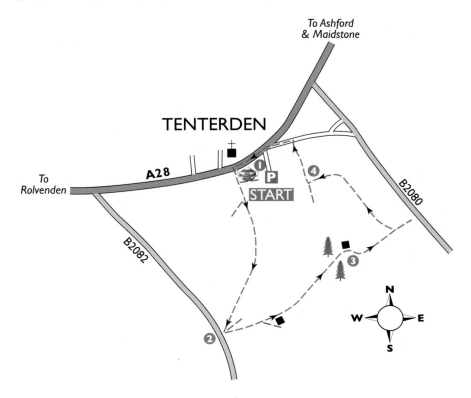

View to St Mildred's Church in Tenterden.

3 Follow the track as it curves right past a converted barn and soon becomes a narrow tarmac road. After 200m, turn left on a grass path behind the gardens of houses. Ahead to the left is a view of a converted oast house, with **Tenterden Church** in the distance. At the end of the field on the left, go straight ahead by some taller trees on a path with a garden fence on the left. Go straight across **Tilden Gill Road** to a footpath sign, then ahead on a stone path between gardens and straight across **Cruttenden Close**. Continue ahead on a tarmac path between fences and straight over another estate road then over a footbridge across a stream and up steps, then between hedges, with an orchard of tall old apple trees on the right.

4 On reaching a T-junction with a wider track turn right. Follow this rough track, finally with a recreation ground on the left and houses on the right, until you reach a road. Turn left alongside the road to reach **Recreation Ground Road**, with its car parks, on the left or continue into the **High Street** to reach **The Lemon Tree**.

Places of Interest Nearby

Kent & East Sussex Railway runs steam trains on a picturesque 10.5-mile line from Tenterden to Bodiam, close to the castle. ⊕ www.kesr.org.uk ☎ 01580 765155.

Bodiam Castle (National Trust) is a fairytale moated castle, over 700 years old. ☎ 01580 830196.

Bodiam Castle.

The war memorial cross on the Downs.

13 LENHAM
4 miles/6.4km

Terrain There are some gradual slopes on this walk and the field paths can be muddy, but there are no stiles.

Map OS Explorer 137 Ashford or 149 Sittingbourne & Faversham.

Starting point The car park in Maidstone Road (GR TQ 898523).

How to get there   Lenham is on the A20 between Maidstone and Ashford. Turn south off the A20 into the village. Stagecoach Bus 10 between Maidstone and Ashford stops in the village square and the railway station is ¾ mile from the square. **Sat nav** ME17 2QH.

The lovely village square in Lenham is surrounded by historic buildings and has a slightly continental feel from the pollarded lime trees. The walk starts near there and takes you up to the North Downs, where you take an ancient pilgrims' trackway past a more recent memorial cross cut into the chalk. The track is lined with colourful and fragrant downland flowers, then the walk returns through sheep pastures and past the ancient church and tithe barn.

The Tea Room

Pippa's Tea Room is housed in a lovely timbered building that dates back to the 15th century, so you are surrounded by beams and old fireplaces. The delicious food includes a selection of hot meals, including pies and all-day breakfasts. There are also cream teas and a variety of cakes and sandwiches. Open 10am-5pm Mon-Sat, 11am-4pm Sun. 01622 851360

Please note that credit cards aren't accepted but you can use a cheque with bank card.

The Walk

1 From the entrance to the car park, turn left for 150m to a T-junction then left again into the village square. As you proceed, the tea room is on the right but, to continue the walk, keep ahead to the left of it, alongside **Faversham Road**. You soon pass the old village gaol on the left, built in the mid-18th century as a workhouse mortuary, then continue for 200m to reach a main road.

2 Cross with care and turn left on the pavement to go past a row of houses. Ignore the first footpath sign just past them but, 70m further on, turn right at a fingerpost to go up steps. Go diagonally left (10 o'clock) across a large field, aiming about 200m left of a silo tower and buildings in the distance. At the far corner of the field go through a gap in a fence, 15m to the right of a telegraph pole, and turn right on a track. You are now on the **North Downs Way** (NDW), which in this area follows the ancient **Pilgrims' Way** to Canterbury. There are wild flowers under the hedge on the left and to the right are views to the higher ground of the **Greensand Ridge**.

3 When you reach a lane on a bend, go straight ahead to the right, taking care as there is no footway. After 200m, the lane bends right but you go straight ahead on the **Pilgrims' Way** at a NDW signpost. Keep ahead on this track where a footpath goes off right and ahead past a vehicle barrier. Soon there is a large cross cut into the chalk downs on the left, a memorial to those who died in the two World Wars. Stay on the track, which now has wide verges that have colourful downland flowers such as thyme, marjoram and yellow bird's-foot trefoil,

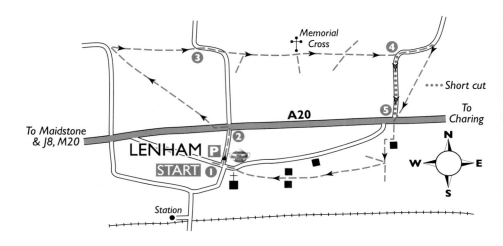

attracting butterflies and other insects in summer. Ignore footpaths going off on both sides, then the track continues through trees, with primroses and other flowers in spring, and later reaches a lane.

4 Here you have a choice – you can turn right and walk along the lane, taking extra care on the bend, until you reach the main road, then follow instructions from Point 5. Alternatively, for a slightly longer walk, go straight ahead on the lane to the left, walking gradually uphill for 400m then turn right at a fingerpost to go through scrub for 10m to a pedestrian gate. Go diagonally right (2 o'clock) across a long field, aiming for a white house. At the far right corner, go through a gap in the hedge with care as it goes onto the lane, then left to the main road.

5 Cross the road with care and go straight ahead on the private drive to **East Lenham**, along an avenue of trees. Where there is a metal gate across the drive go through a pedestrian gate to the right of it. Go sharp left along the left edge of a field alongside a wire fence, soon bending right to a marker post, then left alongside a fence and hedge. Where the hedge ends, go through a pedestrian gate next to a metal gate. Go ahead for 20m then turn right to cross a sheep pasture (keep dogs on lead), walking about 40m from the fence on the right. Cross a stream via a bridge of railway sleepers at a gap in a broken hedge and past a derelict stile then maintain direction across a smaller field to a pedestrian gate. Continue over the next field to a pedestrian gate at the

The old forge cottage by the churchyard.

end of a garden, with a view to the right to the memorial cross on the Downs. Go past the garden and a barn and straight over a drive, then over a footbridge to the left of a pond. Keep to the right edge of a field, passing a small pond and gardens. Ahead of you are the church and a huge tithe barn, both dating from the 14th century. Go through a gate into the churchyard and on a path past the church, with a lovely black and white timbered house on the right. At the end of the churchyard is the village square, with the tea room to the right and the car park along the road straight ahead at the junction.

Place of Interest Nearby

Leeds Castle is a majestic moated castle, with lovely grounds, gardens and birds of prey. ⊕ www.leeds-castle.com ☎ 01622 765400.

The Royal Military Canal at Appledore.

14 APPLEDORE
5 miles/8km

Terrain A fairly flat walk, with no stiles.

Map OS Explorer 125 Romney Marsh

Starting point The car park at the village hall in Appledore (GR TQ 956295).

How to get there Appledore can be reached from the B2080, either from Tenterden or from the A2070 at Brenzett, 10 miles south of Ashford. **Sat nav TN26 2AF.**

The first part of this walk takes you alongside the Royal Military Canal, constructed between 1804 and 1806 as a defence against a feared invasion by Napoleon Bonaparte and his French army. Now it provides a tranquil home for swans and other waterbirds, such as herons, moorhens, coots and kingfishers. The route continues along quiet lanes and through vineyards and sheep pastures to return to the village.

The Tea Room

Miss Mollett's High Class Tea Room lives up to its name, with excellent food in pleasant surroundings. Delicious afternoon teas are served, along with lovely home-made cakes and clotted cream meringues, all with a range of speciality teas to choose from. Light meals and toasted sandwiches are also available. Open 10am-5pm every day in summer and winter weekends, 10am-4pm winter weekdays.

🌐 www.missmollettstearoom.co.uk ☎ 01233 758555.

Please note that credit and debit cards are not accepted.

The Walk

1 If parked in the car park behind the village hall go back out of the entrance and turn right alongside the road. You pass a couple of lovely timbered houses and the tea room. Continue past the **Black Lion** pub and churchyard and keep straight ahead where another road goes off to the right. Follow the road ahead for 200 metres, taking extra care on a section without footway, then go left through a wooden pedestrian

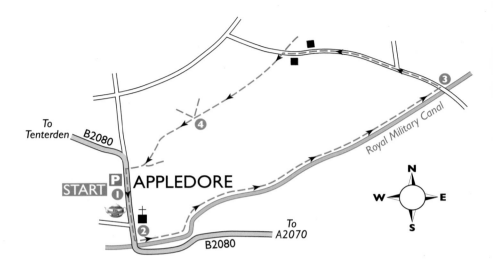

gate and past an information board that shows the wildlife to be found around the **Royal Military Canal**.

❷ The path goes up to the bank of the canal and you follow the grassy bank, or the alternative path that runs parallel to it at a lower level. Be wary of the frequent rabbit holes. The canal is lined by trees, including willows and alders, and there are hawthorn and gorse bushes, while you may see swans, herons and various ducks on the canal, and perhaps even a kingfisher. You pass a later defensive feature in the form of a **World War II pillbox** and there are grapevines in the fields to the left.

❸ After two miles, you reach a minor road near a house. Turn left on the lane and follow it for three quarters of a mile, using the verge when necessary and ignoring a road that goes off right. You pass **Smith's Farmhouse** on the right then, 200m after passing **Bakers Farm** on the left of the road, turn left at a fingerpost and concrete footpath sign to follow a wide path going diagonally right (2 o'clock) through a vineyard. Cross a plank bridge over a ditch near a large ash tree and maintain direction across the next field to go through a wide gap in a hedge. Continue ahead on a wide grassy track through another vineyard then go straight over a rough track to a marker post and straight ahead on another track, with a line of trees on your right.

4 Where the trees end look for a marker post at the corner of a wire fence and go sharp left past a large hump in the field. There is a fine view from here over **Romney Marsh** to **Dungeness power station** and a wind farm in the distance on the left. Follow the grassy track downhill, aiming to the left of a pylon, and at the bottom of the field go through a metal pedestrian gate by a large oak tree. Go ahead across a small meadow, over a footbridge, then diagonally left (10 o'clock) up the next field, aiming towards houses and a telegraph pole. At the top of the field turn sharp left, soon past the gardens of houses. When you reach a tarmac track turn right through a metal gate and follow the track past a recreation ground to a road, then turn left to return to the car park and village tea room.

Place of Interest Nearby

Rare Breeds Centre has farm animals, birds of prey and children's play areas. ⊕ www.rarebreeds.org.uk ☎ 01233 861493

View over vineyards and Romney Marsh.

Boats at Faversham Creek

15 FAVERSHAM

5 miles/8km

Terrain A mainly flat walk, but exposed to north winds and some paths can be wet, no stiles.

Map OS Explorer 149 Sittingbourne & Faversham.

Starting point The car park in Partridge Lane, off North Lane (GR TR 015615).

How to get there Roads lead into Faversham from the A2, near to Junction 6 of the M2. The railway station is ½ mile from the start and there are buses to Faversham from Canterbury, Ashford, Maidstone and the Medway Towns. **Sat nav** ME13 7DX.

This route takes you out of the historic town of Faversham and alongside tidal creeks where you can see restored sailing barges and more modern boats. The creeks and marshes also provide important habitats for birds such as herons, little egrets and many species of waders, plus several rare plants. You return past the tower of a windmill and an ancient church.

The Tea Room

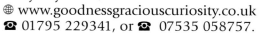

Goodness Gracious Vintage Tea Room in Market Street has a quirky interior, with antiques and curios including vintage china and old photographs around you.
The afternoon teas available include a buffet tea to share and there is a good selection of cakes, as well as pancakes and waffles. It is close to the distinctive Guildhall, parts of which date back to the 16th century. Open 9.30am-6pm every day.

🌐 www.goodnessgraciouscuriosity.co.uk
☎ 01795 229341, or ☎ 07535 058757.

The Walk

1 From the car park walk back to **North Lane**, cross the road with care and turn right under the **Shepherd Neame sign** that goes over the road. After 100m, turn left into **Bridge Road** to cross **Faversham Creek**, where you may see restored sailing barges. Turn immediately right past the creek at a footpath sign for the **Saxon Shore Way**, which is followed for the first part of this walk. Walk between houses and the creek, soon passing the **Albion Taverna** pub then, 200m on, the path bends inland to skirt houses. Where the wall on the right of the path ends go straight ahead for 50m towards terraced houses then right along a paved path by a footpath sign. After a few metres keep ahead on an earth path, with a wall on your right and, after 50m, take the right fork in the path. Where the wall ends, turn right to regain the creek.

2 Turn left along the raised bank alongside the creek, with the **Oyster Stores** building visible on the opposite bank, then later a boatyard

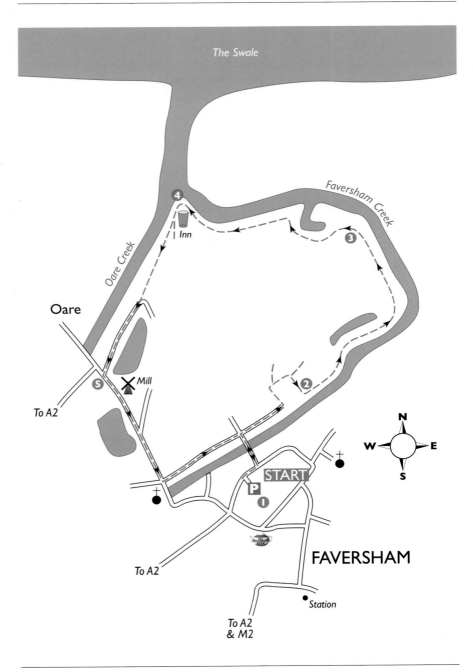

Sailing barges at Faversham Creek.

for yachts. Keep along the raised bank to a kissing gate, then ahead between the creek on the right and a lagoon on the left. Once past the lagoon, keep ahead towards a white house in the distance. On reaching another kissing gate, look back for a view to the distinctive spire of **Faversham Church**. In midsummer, the muddy marshes between the path and the creek are tinged lilac by the flowers of sea lavender, while the lime-green umbel flowers alongside the path are the rare hog's fennel.

3 The path bends left through another kissing gate, with another gate after 50 metres. Soon there are more lagoons on the right, where you may see elegant little egrets searching for fish. The path bends right to reach the main creek, then left towards the masts of sailing boats in the distance. Go through a kissing gate near an abandoned boat then the path bends right towards a house.

4 Continue past the **Shipwright's Arms**, then the path bends left between the inn and a boatyard. The creek here is lined with sailing boats and you may see the yellow flowers of golden samphire on the banks. Go straight over a rough track and ahead on a path between dykes full of reeds on the left and a fence around moorings on the right. On reaching a road on a bend go ahead to the right to walk along the road between **Oare Creek** on the right and a large lake on the left.

5 When you reach a busy road near a T-junction cross with great care and turn left on a path alongside industrial buildings. Continue past **Mill House** on the left, which has the base of a windmill behind it, and keep ahead past side roads, soon with a large lake behind the fence on the right. Keep ahead past **Davington Primary School** and houses to reach **Davington church**, built in 1153 and all that remains of an ancient priory. Go on the pavement to the left of the church but, after 30m, at the top of **Davington Hill**, turn left to cross the road and go ahead along another road, with a wall on the left and allotments on the right (take care, no footway). You pass **Davington Manor** and later industrial buildings. At a T-junction, turn right to cross the creek, then right at the road by the brewery and next left to the car park.

Places of Interest Nearby

The excellent **Fleur de Lis Heritage Centre** in Preston Street has exhibits and information on the local area and its history.

Shepherd Neame Brewery Tours give a chance to look behind the scenes at Britain's oldest brewer and learn how beer is made.
⊕ www.shepherdneame.co.uk ☎ 01795 542016.

Brogdale Collections is the home of the **National Fruit Collection**, with hundreds of varieties of different fruits.
⊕ www.brogdalecollections.org ☎ 01795 536250.

Chilham Castle.

16 CHILHAM
3.5 miles/5.6km

Terrain There are some gradual slopes on this walk and the paths can be muddy, one stile.

Map OS Explorer 137 Ashford or 149 Sittingbourne & Faversham.

Starting point The car park off Taylors Hill or the nearby tea room in the village square (GR TR 066536).

How to get there Chilham is at the junction of the A28 and A252, 6 miles west of Canterbury, with the car park accessed from the A252, ½ mile west of this junction. Chilham railway station is just off the route and Stagecoach buses between Ashford and Canterbury go through the edge of the village. **Sat nav CT4 8BZ.**

Chilham is one of the most attractive villages in the county, with black and white timbered houses clustered around its square, so that it is easy to imagine that you are back in Tudor times. It is no surprise that this scene has featured in several films and period dramas on TV. The walk also takes you past a lovely white-boarded mill and tranquil sections of the Great Stour river. There are also views of the historic house and Norman tower at Chilham Castle.

The Tea Room

Shelly's Tea Rooms occupies one of the lovely timbered houses in the village square, so the interior is redolent of history, with beamed ceilings above you. There is an array of cakes to choose from, or you might be tempted by an all-day breakfast or a hot lunch. However, in such traditional surroundings you might feel that a cream tea is in keeping. Open every day 10am-5pm. ⊕ www.shellystearooms.com ☎ 01227 730303.

The Walk

❶ From the car park on **Taylors Hill**, walk up to the village square. Go past (or into) the tea room on the left to the end of the square near the **White Horse** inn and turn right down **The Street**. Go downhill past more lovely old houses and continue ahead (not right) when you reach the **Woolpack Inn**. Take care as there is no footway for 100m, then keep ahead on the pavement on the left side of the road. Ignore any roads going off left and follow the road as it bends right in front of houses to reach a main road.

2 Cross with care to a narrow road to the left of a garage and go across a railway when the barriers allow. Keep ahead on the road to cross a branch of the river then on a tarmac track with **Chilham Mill** on your left. This well-preserved mill was built in the mid-1800s and operated until 1934. Go over a bridge over the main **Great Stour** then bend left on a rough track. Just before a wooden gate keep left on a path alongside the river then up through trees, with hart's tongue ferns beneath. Go straight across a cross-path and up through more trees then along the left edge of a field, alongside a hedge. Soon there are views along the **Stour Valley** in both directions. At the end of the field go through a gap in trees to a wide track.

3 Turn right on this track to walk beneath trees, including some large beeches. Ignore any side paths as you walk gradually uphill, then later you can see across the valley to **Chilham Castle** on the right, with a couple of large wooden seats from which to admire the view. About 300m past these seats, keep straight ahead at a marker post where

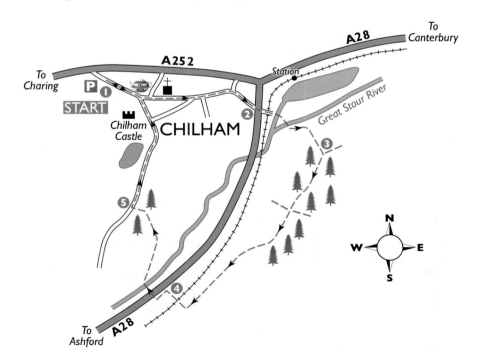

another path goes off right. The path is narrower here, still between trees, and there is a bank on the left. After another quarter of a mile, you reach a cross-track by metal gates and a telegraph pole. Turn right here to go under the railway and past houses to a main road.

4 Turn left along the roadside verge for 80m, then cross with care to a wooden pedestrian gate and a footbridge over the river. Go diagonally right across a long field, aiming for the mansion in the distance. After 400m, go through a wooden kissing gate at the far left corner of the field and ahead on the left side of the next field for 200m then left over a stile in the fenceline. Go up steps and diagonally right (2 o'clock) across a field to the mid-point of a small wood, then ahead on a path through trees and between gardens to a road.

5 Turn right along the road, soon passing two lovely black and white timbered houses. On the left are the grounds of **Chilham Castle**, with a large lake. Where the road bends right at a junction go left up the steep **School Hill** to return to the village square.

Places of Interest Nearby

The nearby city of **Canterbury** has several attractions, including **the cathedral**, **Roman Museum**, **Canterbury Tales** and **Beaney House Museum**.

Chilham Mill and Great Stour river.

Princes Parade at Hythe.

17 HYTHE

2.75 or 4.25 miles/4.4 or 6.8km

Terrain This is a flat walk, entirely on good surfaces and with no stiles.

Map OS Explorer 138 Dover, Folkestone & Hythe.

Starting point The tea room is at 126 High Street. There are several car parks in Hythe but the most convenient is The Paddocks pay & display in Prospect Road (GR TR 162347).

How to get there Hythe is on the A259 and can be reached via the A261 from Junction 11 of the M20. Stagecoach buses from Ashford and Folkestone serve the town. **Sat nav CT21 5NN.**

This walk has a winning combination of a stretch alongside the tree-lined Royal Military Canal, with its water-loving birds and plants, followed by a glorious return section alongside the sea. There are wonderful views along the coast and across the English Channel as you return to Hythe, with its attractive buildings and gardens, and historic church.

The Tea Room _____

Tea & Tides has Dutch specialities such as a delicious apple cake and fluffy pancakes in addition to a range of cakes, breakfasts, hot lunches and lighter snacks. It is situated in the High Street,

which has many old buildings including the columned Town Hall, built in 1794. Open seven days a week 9am-4pm. ☎ 01303 262426.

The Walk

1 With your back to the **Tea & Tides café** turn right for 10m then right again down the narrow **Theatre Street** to reach a main road. Turn right alongside it for 100m, then cross it at a pedestrian crossing and go ahead to the bank of the **Royal Military Canal**. Turn left on one of the paths that run parallel to the canal. On reaching a road (**Twiss Road**) go straight across to a wide tarmac path by a bridleway fingerpost.

2 Continue past a barrier and **Royal Military Canal** sign. You have the choice of walking along the lower gravel-surfaced track or the upper grassy path on the bank of the canal. After a quarter of a mile, a green bridge crosses the canal on the right, providing the first opportunity for a short cut, but otherwise continue ahead past a small picnic area. About a quarter of a mile further on, another footbridge over the canal provides a second chance for a short cut to the promenade but the full

The Royal Military Canal at Hythe.

walk keeps straight ahead. Later the path passes another picnic area and a third bridge then finally passes a school on the left and curves left to a main road.

3 Turn right alongside the road to pass an information board for the **Seabrook Outfall** then continue past modern apartments and turn right on a short road to a T-junction. Cross with care to the promenade at the end of **Sandgate Bay**. There are views to the left to **Sandgate** and **Folkestone** but the walk continues to the right, along the promenade between the shingle beach on the left and a road on the right. As you walk there are views across the **English Channel** to the **French coast** and ahead, to the left, to **Dungeness Power Station**. As the buildings on **Hythe** seafront get closer you may spot **Hythe Church** on higher ground to their right.

4 Continue on the promenade past the **Hythe Imperial** hotel, then houses and a small café but 400m on, immediately before the **Hythe & Saltwood Sailing Club**, turn right on a path next to a blue metal gate with gold anchors. After 80m, cross a road to a wide tarmac track

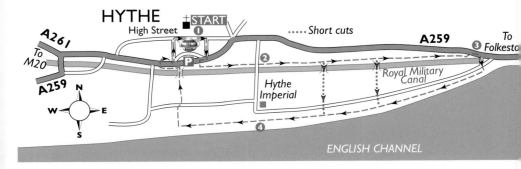

called **Ladies Walk** and go ahead past tennis courts and later a cricket pitch to reach a bridge over the canal, with a fine view of **Hythe Church** ahead. Cross the bridge and turn left, then just before the next bridge turn right to cross the main road at a pedestrian crossing. Turn right for 20m, then left into **Prospect Road** and follow it for 100m back to the **High Street** then go right to return to the café.

Places of Interest Nearby

Romney, Hythe and Dymchurch Railway has a-third-of-full-size steam trains running for 13.5 miles across Romney Marsh. ⊕ www.rhdr.org.uk ☎ 01797 362353.

Port Lympne Reserve provides the opportunity to go on safari to see free-roaming lions, rhinos, giraffes and other large animals. ⊕ www.aspinallfoundation.org/portlympne ☎ 01303 264647.

View to Reculver Towers.

18 HERNE BAY

3.5, 6.5 or 8 miles/5.6, 10.4 or 12.8km

Terrain Some gradual slopes, muddy field paths and one stile on the longest route; shortest route flat.

Map OS Explorer 150 Canterbury & Isle of Thanet.

Starting point The clock tower on the promenade (GR TR 177684). There are several car parks in Herne Bay, the most convenient being in Beach Street or Market Street.

How to get there Herne Bay is reached by roads off the A299 or A2990. The railway station is ¾ mile from the start and there are frequent Stagecoach buses from Canterbury. Sat nav CT6 5PL (Beach Street) or CT6 5PP (Market Street).

There are superb sea views on this bracing walk, with large ships and the huge turbines of a wind farm. There is the option of walking as far as the iconic towers at Reculver, visible for miles from land and sea. Here are the atmospheric remains of the long-abandoned church, plus the walls of a Roman fort. An optional inland loop takes you past the tower of a windmill.

The Tea Room

The **Vintage Empire** is at 104 High Street, near the junction with Beach Street, and here you can step back in time to the 1940s as that era has been lovingly recreated. The bone china, knitted tea cosies, embroidered tablecloths, old books and newspapers, plus the vintage dresses of the waitresses, all add

to the period atmosphere, and even the menu looks like a ration book. There are delicious afternoon teas, a selection of cakes and light lunches such as homemade quiche or giant scotch eggs. Open 10am-4pm every day.

☎ 01227 360258

Please note that debit and credit cards are not taken.

The Walk

1 Starting at the clock tower on the promenade and facing the sea, turn right along the promenade. You pass some attractive houses on the right, the **Ship Inn**, **King's Hall** and later the sailing club. Continue along the promenade for a mile and a half, with views across the sea to wind farms and large ships and ahead to the towers at **Reculver**, while on the right are grassy slopes, colourful with wild flowers in summer.

2 About 100m before the end of the wider section of the promenade you have the option of retracing your steps back to the town (walk distance = 3.5 miles) but to continue towards **Reculver** turn right up a wide concrete track by an information board for the **Coastal Park** at **Bishopstone**. Continue around a bend in the track to reach a small car park but turn sharp left before it at a sign for the **National Cycle Network**. Go past an information board for **Reculver Country Park** then, 40m on, at a T-junction with another path, turn left and go straight on to cross a footbridge. Over the bridge turn left and straight on behind gardens, then between trees, ignoring any paths going off to the sides. At a cross-path with steps turn right, now with houses on the right and sea views to the left. The concrete path ends at steps up to a grassy area and small car park.

3 Go sharp left across the grassy area, close to the cliffs, and ahead through a gap in bushes for 20m to an extensive grassy area on top of the cliffs and views ahead to the towers at **Reculver**. Keep ahead on the grassy paths, being aware of the drop from cliffs on the left. In summer you may see sand martins, which nest in holes in the soft cliffs. When you reach **Reculver** there is a café and toilets, plus a children's playground.

4 You could retrace your steps back from here to Point 3, then follow instructions from Point 6 (walk distance = 6.5 miles). However, to do an additional inland loop keep left of the playground to a pub then turn right along a road for 30m, taking care as there is no footway. Turn left on a concrete track in front of another café, which soon bends right past a caravan park and becomes a rough track. Where the caravans on the right end go sharp right in front of a metal gate across the track to walk on the right edge of a field, with a ditch and tall poplars on your

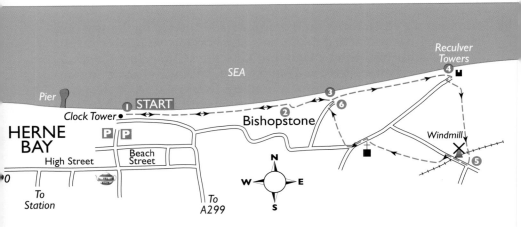

right. Where the ditch goes off to the right keep straight ahead across the field, towards a windmill in the distance. Keep ahead on the right edge of a field, with a reed-filled ditch on the right, cross a footbridge over a ditch, and continue ahead, still with a ditch on the right. At the end of the field go over a stile to the right of a metal gate then right on a concrete track for 20m, then left to go under a railway. Keep ahead on a track that goes gradually uphill towards a windmill.

5 On reaching a road turn right along it, later crossing a bridge over the railway then, 100m on, just before farm buildings on the right, go left on a rough track at a fingerpost. After 300m, turn right near houses on a path through trees to a pedestrian gate then turn right to cross a footbridge. Go up steps, then diagonally left (10 o'clock) across a long field, aiming for a church in the distance. Cross another footbridge at the end of the first field then maintain direction across a smaller field to a fingerpost to the right of the church. Turn left along the road, taking care as there is no footway, and keep right where it forks by a thatched house. You reach a T-junction then, 10m on, turn right through a gap in the hedge and on the right side of a field, next to a tall hedge. At the corner of the hedge, keep ahead across the field, aiming for the right-hand house of a line. Cross a ditch and maintain direction to reach a road. Turn right for 50m to a small car park and go sharp left to the far corner of the grassy area crossed on the outward journey.

View to Herne Bay and Isle of Sheppey.

6 Go left (right if returning from Reculver) down steps and on a concrete path, soon with views ahead to **Herne Bay** and the **Isle of Sheppey**. Part of the way down the next flight of steps turn left by a marker post to go on a path through scrub, then behind gardens. Keep straight ahead to cross the footbridge over **Bishopstone Glen** and keep straight on, ignoring a path on the left, but 15m after the bridge turn right on a wider tarmac path. After 40m, go past a small car park to the wide concrete track and turn right to go down to the promenade then left to return to the start, with views to the town as you walk.

Place of Interest Nearby

Wildwood, 4 miles south of Herne Bay, has over 200 native British animals, including otters and red squirrels, and an adventure playground. ⊕ www.wildwoodtrust.org ☎ 01227 712111.

Viking Bay at Broadstairs

19 BROADSTAIRS
1.75 or 3.5 miles/2.8 or 5.6km

Terrain The entire route is on tarmac or grass and is mainly flat, with no stiles.

Map OS Explorer 150 Canterbury & Isle of Thanet.

Starting point The car park in Albion Street or the tea room in the same road (GR TR 398679).

How to get there Broadstairs is reached on the A255, which links to the A299 near Ramsgate. The railway station is ½ mile from the start and there are frequent buses from Ramsgate and Margate. Sat nav CT10 1NE.

Offering you lovely sea views and the chance to visit great sandy beaches, this walk is suitable for any time of year as it is entirely on surfaced paths. There is the option of a shorter walk, or a longer one with a section through a pleasant park, while the return part of either route runs close to the beach and sea and beneath white chalk cliffs.

The Tea Room

Bessie's Tea Parlour at 45 Albion Street has a lovely vintage feel, with the background music, floral tablecloths, bone china and chandeliers adding to the atmosphere. There is local produce on offer, such as Kingcott Dairy Kentish blue cheese served with pear and walnut chutney or with leek in a tart. You can also savour Kentish huffkins with a variety of fillings and, reflecting the coastal location, a crab sandwich or lobster brioche. Several tempting cakes are also on offer, along with a choice of afternoon teas. Open 10am-5pm Mon-Fri, 10am-6pm Sat & Sun.

⊕ www.bessiesteaparlour.co.uk
☎ 01843 600189.

The Walk

1 From the **Albion Street car park** turn right along **Albion Street** to soon reach the tea room. From there cross the road and continue alongside it for 50m then turn left through a small garden to reach the promenade above cliffs and the main beach, **Viking Bay**. Turn right along the promenade to walk away from the harbour and small pier and continue until you reach an area with a bandstand. Skirt this on the seaward side, passing a small ornate clock tower on your left. The tarmac path bends right between the fence above the cliff on the left and a grassy area on the right, then you turn left over a footbridge across a road that goes down to the beach.

2 Continue ahead past the **Louisa Bay apartments** on a path of paving

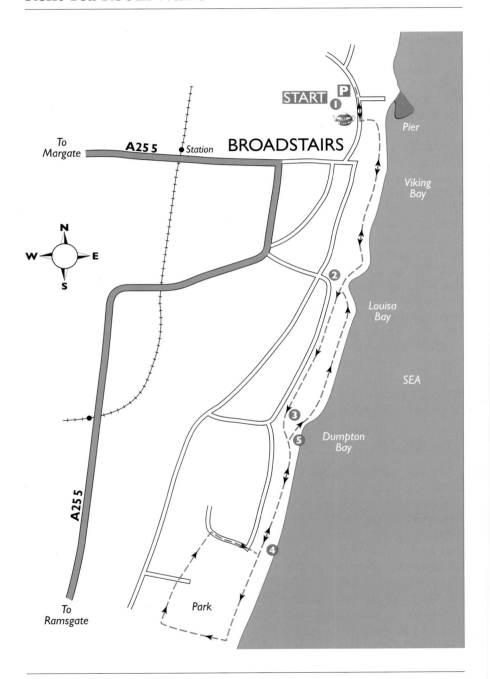

slabs, now with a road on the right and great sea views on the left over another beach, and also back to **Broadstairs harbour**. Soon there are views ahead towards **Dumpton Bay** in the foreground and **Pegwell Bay** in the distance, and the path bends right to reach a road junction.

❸ *For the shorter walk*, go sharp left here down a tarmac track at a footpath sign then left at the bottom (instructions from Point 5) but *for the longer walk*, which continues above the cliffs, keep left across this track and on a narrower tarmac path across a grassy area to a wire fence and line of bushes on top of the cliffs. Continue ahead alongside the fence, now walking gradually uphill on a grassy area alongside the fence, and with more sea views as the bushes end on the left.

❹ Where the grass ends at a line of bollards and the road on the right bends inland, go straight ahead on a tarmac path, signed **National Cycle Network**, so beware of bicycles. Pass a tall white house with a turret, then the wide path goes between trees on both sides as it enters the **Victoria Memorial Park**. Here you will hear the squawks of ring-necked parakeets and perhaps spot one of these bright green birds, adding an exotic touch to the walk. Exit the park via metal gates, just past a refreshment kiosk, then go immediately sharp right, away from the sea on a tarmac path between walls. After 300m, the path bends sharp right, now with a fence on the right and the park beyond it. Continue ahead on this path past two cul-de-sac roads on the left until you reach a road near tennis courts. If you require refreshment at this point turn right on a rough road for 50m, enter the park through a metal gate then, after 80m, go left on a tarmac path to reach the tea room at the restored **Victorian Glasshouse** (check opening times). Otherwise the walk continues by going straight across the road and ahead with the tennis courts on your left and a flint wall on the right. Keep ahead on this path for 400m, later with a brick wall on your right, until you reach a wide road and turn right towards the sea. At a T-junction, cross to regain the grassy area and turn left to retrace your steps from the outward journey.

❺ At a road junction, turn right down a tarmac track past a yellow and black gate towards the beach at **Dumpton Gap** (toilets here). (If the tide and waves are particularly high, retrace your steps back along the top of the cliffs instead.) On reaching the concrete apron alongside the beach turn left past a small café and ahead alongside tall white cliffs of chalk with lines of flints and plants such as pink valerian. On reaching the next café you can continue past it to the main beach and the lift to the upper promenade. Otherwise walk up the concrete ramp to the left of the café, under the footbridge, and up steps on the right. From there retrace your steps along the promenade and back to **Albion Street**.

Places of Interest Nearby

There is the **Dickens House Museum** in Broadstairs and, in Margate, the **Turner Contemporary** art gallery and the large **Dreamland** amusement park.

Dumpton Bay.

View to St Margaret's Bay.

20 ST MARGARET'S BAY
2.5 miles/4km

Terrain   There are some gradual slopes and some of the paths are stony, but no stiles.

Map   OS Explorer 138 Dover, Folkestone & Hythe.

Starting point   The pay and display car park at the bottom of Bay Hill, St Margaret's Bay (GR TR 369446).

How to get there   St Margaret's Bay is 3 miles north-east of Dover and can be reached on B roads from the A258 and running through St Margaret's-at-Cliffe. Sat nav CT15 6DX.

This walk has wonderful views across the English Channel, with the French coast visible on clear days. You can watch the ferries going in and out of Dover harbour and other ships passing through the Channel. There are also colourful flowers and butterflies to admire on the chalk grassland and views of the white cliffs. The route takes you to the attractive, white-painted lighthouse at South Foreland, built in 1793 and used by Marconi for the first international radio transmission in 1899.

The Tea Room

Mrs Knott's Tea Room is within the South Foreland lighthouse, now managed by the National Trust, but you can also sit outside and gaze out over the English Channel. The interior has vintage-style wallpaper and furniture, including a chiming clock and old gramophone and you can tuck into scrumptious cakes and cream teas. Open seven days a week late March to late October 11am-5pm, weekends only early Feb-late March 11am-3pm, closed Nov-Jan. ☎ 01304 853281. When this tea room is closed there are good alternatives at **The Pines** (passed on the walk) or by car at **Shelly's** at the top of Bay Hill.

Mrs Knott's Tea Room at South Foreland Lighthouse.

The Walk

① From the car park behind the beach, walk back up the road, taking great care as there is no footway. Where the road bends sharply right go left on a tarmac track, signed to **The Pines Garden**. At a fork in the track keep left to go past **The Pines Garden Tea Room & Museum**, then the track climbs gradually, with **The Pines Garden** on the right.

② At the top of the incline, go straight over a cross-track and through a pedestrian gate to the right of a cattle grid. Follow the narrow earth track, with a tall bank of chalk grassland, colourful with flowers

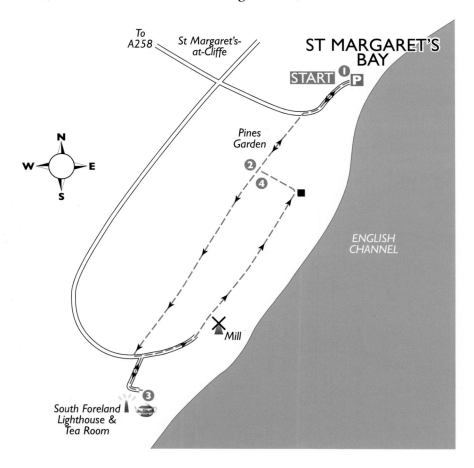

in summer, on your left. The track goes between bushes and trees, through another gate next to a cattle grid, then gradually uphill between trees. After going through a third gate alongside a grid, keep ahead between a wire fence and bushes on the left and more bushes on the right. Where there is a seat on the right, look back for a view to **St Margaret's**. Go through another gate alongside a grid and straight over a rough track, then ahead on a tarmac track for 100m and left to the entrance to the lighthouse and tea room.

3 You can see inside the lighthouse and there is the opportunity to walk down to the cliffs for views of the **White Cliffs** and **Dover Harbour** and over the **English Channel**. However, be very careful, especially if you have children or dogs with you, as there are sheer drops from the cliff edge. After your visit, retrace your steps from the lighthouse by turning left for 30m from the gate to the staff car park, then right on the tarmac road to reach the rough track you crossed on the outward journey. Turn right on this track and after a few metres there are views ahead to **St Margaret's Bay** and the tower of a disused windmill, and over the sea on the right. The wide chalky track goes past the garden of the windmill, then **Lighthouse Down nature reserve** on the right. The reserve is home to colourful downland flowers such as harebells and

The beach at St Margaret's Bay.

Dover Castle.

knapweed and lovely blue butterflies. Continue ahead past cottages on the left and through a gate to the left of a cattle grid, with views ahead to **St Margaret's Bay** and the obelisk that is the memorial to the Dover Patrol. Go gradually downhill, past another grid, and near a white bungalow, bend sharp left on the track for 200m to reach a T-junction with a cross-track.

4 Turn right on the rough track to retrace your steps past **The Pines Garden and Tea Room** to the road and turn right to reach the car park.

Place of Interest Nearby

Dover Castle (English Heritage) is one of the most famous castles in England and a landmark on the coast, where it has guarded the entrance to Dover harbour for hundreds of years. You can also explore secret tunnels from World War II.
⊕ www.english-heritage.org.uk/dover ☎ 01304 211067.

OTHER TITLES FROM COUNTRYSIDE BOOKS

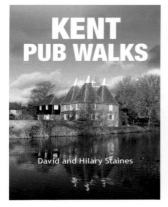

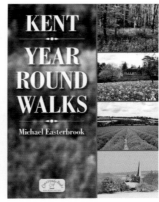

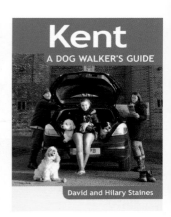

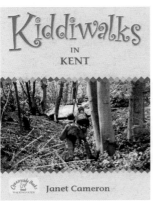

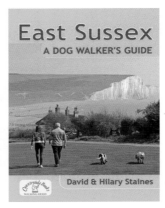

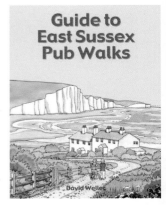

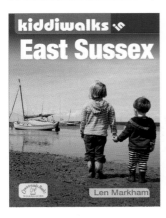

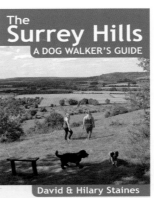

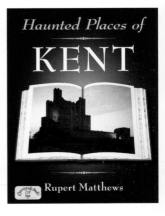

To see the full range of books by Countryside Books please visit
www.countrysidebooks.co.uk

Follow us on